The year 1992 sees the Yugoslav situation still unresolved where thousands have died in a bloody civil war. It started in 1989, the year that the communist governments in six Eastern European countries fell in quick succession because they had failed to give their people a modern economy and a just society. These changes were achieved with little bloodshed except in Romania – where hundreds died – and Yugoslavia.

The countries of Eastern Europe are East Germany, Poland, Czechoslovakia, Hungary, Bulgaria, Romania, Yugoslavia and Albania. They are bounded to the north by the Baltic Sea and to the south by the Mediterranean. East Germany and Poland lie on the North German Plain and are mainly flat. Czechoslovakia has the Carpathian mountains within its territory which divide Eastern Europe into north and south. Hungary lies on a plain which has rich agricultural land, while Bulgaria, Yugoslavia, Albania and Romania are very mountainous.

Until 1989 all of these countries had some form of communist government. This meant that the governments ran and owned most of the factories, mines and farms. Today this is all changing as the new governments try to introduce a market economy where industry and agriculture are run by private individuals in response to what the market (the people buying goods) dictates.

Since the end of the Second World War Europe has been divided into a communist east and a democratic west. At the end of the war the British prime minister, Winston Churchill, talked about "an iron curtain" being drawn across Europe. For the next 40 years the Soviet Union maintained its domination of Eastern Europe.

The revolutions of 1989 came about mainly because the Soviet Union allowed them to happen. The Soviet leader, Mikhail Gorbachev, made it plain that the Soviets were changing their communist system and that this meant relations with Eastern Europe would change. In 1989 the peoples of Eastern Europe took him at his word and the communist regimes tumbled.

Before 1945 many countries of Eastern Europe would have described themselves as part of Central Europe. Today they seek to align themselves with Western Europe. East and West Germany are one nation again. And the other countries want close economic ties with the 12 countries of the European Community. This "new Europe" faces great economic and social challenges before it can enjoy peace and prosperity.

Empires and nations

For centuries Eastern Europe has been dominated by neighbouring empires. After the First World War small nation-states were set up as a buffer between Germany and Soviet Russia. After the Second World War Soviet Russia gained control over Eastern Europe.

Early this century Eastern Europe was the battleground of nationalism. The German and Russian empires dominated other nationalities, such as the Poles, Hungarians, Czechs, Croats and many others. Traditionally, four empires had dominated this area: the German Reich, the Austro-Hungarian monarchy, the Ottoman (Turkish) empire and the Russian empire. With the exception of the German Reich, the other empires were visibly in decline. They were weakened by the long struggle for power of the different nationalities within them.

Austria-Hungary

The Austro-Hungarian monarchy was desperately trying to sort out the "national problem" after a century of struggle. As its name indicated, the Austrian Germans and Hungarians shared power within the monarchy, for they were the first national groups to become conscious of belonging to a nation. The Austrian and Hungarian social elites – the landowners and aristocracy – gained political power in the 19th century. They got their power from the ruling Habsburg emperors, who used the leading members of the elite as their advisers.

△ The map above shows how Eastern Europe was divided up between the German, Russian and Austro-Hungarian empires in 1914. A few countries in the Balkans had gained their independence but they were allied to their neighbours.

HOTSPOTS

EASTERN EUROPE
THE ROAD TO DEMOCRACY

JOHN BRADLEY

A GLOUCESTER PRESS BOOK

Contents

▷ East German troops look down on West Germans from the Berlin Wall, 1989. For some 28 years the Berlin Wall symbolised the division of Europe into east and west. It was built by the East German government in 1961 to stop East Germans leaving their country for West Germany. In 1989 many East Germans left their country by crossing the border from Hungary to Austria. In November 1989 the East German government realised they could not stop the flow of people westwards, so they decided to knock down the wall. The old divisions had become meaningless and shortly afterwards the communist leadership resigned.

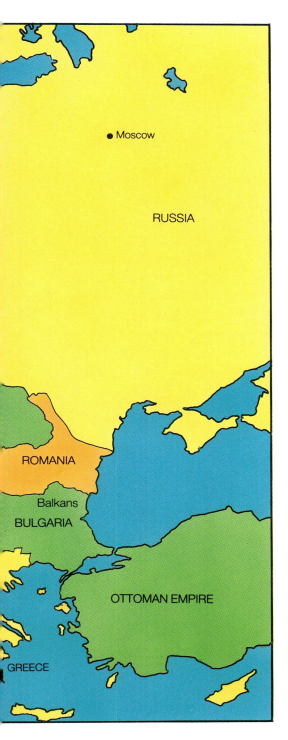

By 1900 numerous other nationalities, at varied stages of political and economic development, were clamouring for greater power within the monarchy: the Czechs, Slovaks, Slovenes, Jews, Ruthenians, Croats, Serbs, Macedonians, Romanians and Poles. (In the 18th century Poland lost its independence and was partitioned among the three great powers, Russia, Germany and Austria-Hungary.) The Habsburgs were giving the Polish aristocracy more positions than the other groups. This encouraged the Poles, who wanted to gain the leadership of the Slav majority within the monarchy. By 1914 the various nationalities realised that none of them could dominate the others for control of the empire, and this did much to undermine the Habsburg emperor.

The Balkans

The Turkish (Ottoman) empire was at the height of its power in the 16th century. In 1683 the Turks laid siege to Vienna but were defeated by the Polish armies. They ruled the part of Eastern Europe known as the Balkans. By 1914 the Ottoman empire had given up large parts of the Balkans and the various nationalities within that area had become independent or semi-independent.

Serbia became an independent kingdom in 1882 and Romania in 1877. The tiny kingdom of Montenegro, proudly free, had never been conquered by the Turks. Albania became an independent Muslim kingdom after the Balkan wars of 1912-13. Bulgaria was created by the Russian Army in 1878, but its independence was only recognised in 1908. A German minor prince then made it a German satellite. Similarly, Romania, Serbia and Montenegro were Russian satellites.

In the Balkans the struggles of nationalities made the balance of power in the area extremely precarious. The Balkan problem concerned the politicians of Europe. They were anxious that no one power should dominate the area. The great powers were involved in complicated alliances to make sure that the balance of power in Europe remained stable. Britain, France and Russia were allied together, while Germany and Austria-Hungary also had treaties. The whole system disintegrated in 1914 when a disgruntled Serbian nationalist assassinated the heir to the Austro-Hungarian throne. Within weeks the two blocs of allies were at war with each other. The shock of the great war, which lasted from 1914-1918, swept away the old empires of Central Europe.

△ Czar Nicholas II was the last emperor of the Russian empire. He ruled the vast empire by following the practice of other czars – using repression and the secret police. In 1917 he was deposed in a revolution.

The Russian empire

The Russian empire was known as the prison of nationalities not only because it violently persecuted them, but also because it tried to make them Russian. The Georgians and Armenians in the Caucasus fiercely resisted Russianisation, as well as the Poles, who assassinated the liberal Czar Alexander II in 1881. The Poles led the fight against the Russians.

Poles within the German Reich had a relatively free political life and enjoyed economic benefits denied the Russian Poles. In Russia, ethnic groups were often uprooted by deportations, or forced to live in vast ghettos. They did not benefit from Russian economic development, and there was no hope of greater political freedom for them or any Russians. They were also persecuted by *pogroms* – semi-official attacks on unarmed civilians which resulted in many deaths. Many of those persecuted, such as the Jews, fled from the country. It was a miracle that the empire did not disintegrate in 1905, following a revolution which was crushed. However, the First World War ensured the destruction of the Russian empire. The Russians lost heart in the war and in 1917 two revolutions took place.

The map shows the results of the Treaty of Versailles. Germany was divided into two: Germany and East Prussia. This gave Poland access to the sea. Czechoslovakia and Yugoslavia were created when different nationalities joined together. Austria and Hungary became small, independent states and Romania gained territory from Hungary and Russia because it had sided with the winners in the First World War.

◁ Austrian police arrest Serbian nationalist, Gavrilo Princip. He had just assassinated the heir to the Austro-Hungarian throne, Archduke Franz Ferdinand. Austria-Hungary declared war on Serbia, which was allied with Russia. This led to the outbreak of the First World War in 1914.

The aftermath of the First World War

The four empires of Central and Eastern Europe emerged from the war defeated and in chaos. This left the nationalities free to become independent without much struggle. Even so the nationalities needed the support of other powers, such as France, Britain and the United States, to guarantee their independence. The problem of frustrated nationalisms was seen as the cause of the terrible suffering and loss of life in the First World War. The Treaty of Versailles was supposed to ensure such a devastating war would never happen again by giving the different nationalities their independence. France, Britain and the United States hoped that giving the peoples of Central and Eastern Europe self-determination, or the right to decide for themselves how they should be governed, would solve the ethnic problems of the area. Because Germany had been an aggressor in the First World War, the new formation of Central Europe would exclude it and act as a buffer between Germany and Soviet Russia.

New, often tiny, states emerged and sometimes disappeared again. German Austria and Hungary became independent republics with practically no ethnic minorities. The Poles broke away from the three defeated empires and formed an independent Poland. Czechs and Slovaks joined together to create Czechoslovakia, while Serbs, Croats and Slovenes formed the independent kingdom of Yugoslavia. Romania benefitted most from the collapse of the empires and annexed large chunks of Russian, Hungarian and Bulgarian territory. Ruthenia joined Czechoslovakia, and the Ukraine, after a short period of independence, was in turn divided between the emerging Soviet Russia and Poland.

It seemed a great achievement to the nationalists of the region to gain independence, but in reality they were only benefitting from the temporary decline of German and Russian power. The problem was that the new states inherited all the ethnic problems of the old Austro-Hungarian empire, which made them extremely unstable. Also there was no tradition of democracy, so many of the states had more than 20 political parties and were ruled by generals rather than political leaders. There was a great deal of political unrest and many politicians were assassinated. With the exception of Czechoslovakia, the economies of the new Eastern European nations were backward, and independence did not fulfill the people's hopes and dreams of prosperity.

The Third Reich

In 1933, the National Socialist leader Adolf Hitler came to power in Germany and created the Third Reich. All the ethnic problems and conflicts of the region came to a head. Hitler not only wanted to regain the territory Germany had lost after the First World War but he also wanted to expand eastwards and gain more living space for Germany. He moved cautiously at first and exploited all the ethnic problems of his neighbours. He encouraged German minorities to assert themselves all over Eastern Europe. In 1938 he peacefully annexed his native Austria.

Later that year he gained the Sudeten German part of Czechoslovakia with the Munich Agreement, signed by Britain and France. Both Britain and France went back on their promise to Czechoslovakia that they would guarantee its independence. In March 1939, under pressure from Hitler, Czechoslovakia collapsed, as Slovaks opted for independence, and Czechs were forced into Hitler's Reich.

The Second World War

In 1939 Hitler signed a non-aggression pact with Josef Stalin of the Soviet Union. A secret clause agreeing to its partition spelled the ruin of Poland. In September German troops invaded Poland. Hitler's and Stalin's armies conquered and divided the unfortunate country between them; only a small territory around Warsaw was left as Poland (under German occupation). France and Britain stood by their promises to Poland and declared war on Hitler's Germany, though not on the Soviet Union.

△ Hitler visits Austria in triumph. In 1938 his army marched into Austria to unite it with Germany.

▽ The British prime minister, Neville Chamberlain, hails the result of the Munich Agreement as "peace in our time". Within a year Europe was at war.

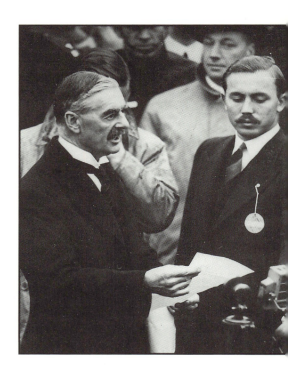

As a result of the same treaty the Soviet Union annexed Bukovina and Moldavia, provinces of Romania, and the Baltic states (Lithuania, Latvia and Estonia). Albania was seized by Germany's ally, Italy, and the Bulgarians joined sides with Germany and Italy to obtain Dobrudja from Romania. The Hungarians also joined Germany and Italy and stirred up trouble in Yugoslavia and Romania in order to regain bits of territory lost after the First World War. In 1941, after the German invasion, Yugoslavia split into three: Serbs, Croats and Slovenes began fighting each other vigorously. The Croatian *Ustashas* launched an extermination campaign against the Serbs, while communist partisans fought against all of them.

Some historians go as far as to claim that the Second World War in Eastern Europe was an ethnic war, not a conflict between democratic Western Europe and fascist Germany and Italy. In 1941 after Hitler's invasion of Soviet Russia, all the European countries under Nazi occupation had to send armies to fight against the Soviet Union, and suffered great loss of life. Hitler also decided to rid Europe of Jews and at least six million Jews are thought to have died as a result. The Soviet Union lost approximately 46 million people during the Second World War. It is thought that at least three million Poles and three million Polish Jews died. Some three million Germans died, along with one and a half million Yugoslavs and many others from the other Eastern European countries.

The Katyn massacres
In April 1943 the Nazis announced that they had discovered a mass grave of Polish prisoners of war in the Katyn Woods. They blamed the Soviets for carrying out this crime. Some 4,000 generals and officers, the "flower of the Polish Army", had been killed. For years the Soviets denied any involvement but in 1990 the Soviet government finally admitted that this was "one of the gravest crimes of Stalinism".

▽ A German soldier takes Polish prisoners into captivity, September 1939. Poland was divided between Germany and Russia and both sides committed many atrocities against the Poles. However, during the war many Polish people joined in the Nazi persecution of the Jews.

The communist stranglehold

After the Second World War, the Soviet armies occupied Eastern Europe. Within a few years those countries had communist one-party systems imposed by Stalin.

△ The Big Three at Yalta, February 1945: the British prime minister, Winston Churchill (left), the American president, Franklin Roosevelt (centre), and the Soviet leader, Josef Stalin (right). The three leaders agreed that "free and unfettered" elections would be held in all the countries freed from Nazi German rule.

Before the end of the war, Stalin met the American president, Franklin Roosevelt, and the British leader, Winston Churchill, in Yalta to discuss the post-war future of Europe. Britain and the United States agreed that democratic governments should be set up in Central and Eastern Europe, but there was little that they could do to enforce this since the Soviet Army controlled those territories. Stalin was able to impose his will on these once proud national states.

After the war, in 1945, Stalin was all-powerful in Eastern Europe. The Soviet Army occupied Poland, Bulgaria, Romania, Hungary, Austria, Czechoslovakia and Berlin, the capital city of Germany. Both Yugoslavia and Albania managed to liberate themselves. Stalin took Ruthenia from Czechoslovakia and added it to the Ukraine. The Baltic states, Bukovina and Moldavia, and all the territories which had been granted to him as concessions by the Nazis, including eastern Poland, were again seized and became part of the Soviet Union. Romania lost two provinces to the Soviet Union, but gained back the Dobrudja territory from Bulgaria. Poland was given big chunks of East German territory, Silesia and Pomerania, but East Prussia became part of the Soviet Union. Yugoslavia was again united under the communist leader Tito. Albania had already liberated itself after the fall and withdrawal of Mussolini's Italy.

The death throes of nationalism

Nationalist, anti-German feelings triumphed at the end of the war. Czechoslovakia expelled the three million-strong German minority in the Sudetenland; in Hungary, Romania and Yugoslavia several hundred thousand Germans were sent to Germany; and in Poland, which now included large parts of German territory, some six million Germans were forced to leave their homes.

However, the war seemed to have exhausted other nationalist aspirations and only the Ukrainian nationalists continued their struggle for independence against the Soviet Army until 1947. Stalin and the threat of communism also kept in check the rivalry between Poles and Czechs; Slovaks and Hungarians; Austrians and Romanians; and Yugoslavs and Bulgarians. Although there were many outstanding ethnic problems, such as the sizeable Hungarian minority in Romania, these were put aside. Many of the Eastern European countries realised that co-operation against Stalin might make them stronger.

Stalin's new order

Stalin was quite indifferent towards this desire for peaceful co-existence of rival nationalities. He wanted to dominate Eastern Europe in order to have a buffer zone between Russia and Germany. He took immediate steps to achieve this ambition.

According to the Yalta Agreement, signed with the United States and Britain in February 1945, he was supposed to hold free elections in all the countries that had been liberated from Nazi Germany. But from the beginning he was determined to make those countries Soviet satellites, even if it meant that he had to falsify the election results. The Soviet Army installed local communist parties in power, and proceeded to ensure that they remained in power by arresting and persecuting their political opponents and manipulating the elections. The Eastern European communists were then invited to join "voluntarily" Stalin's security system, which was later called the Warsaw Pact Alliance.

There were two exceptions to this rule: Finland and Czechoslovakia. Both were allowed to run their own internal affairs as long as they allowed the Soviet Union to direct their foreign policies and remained allied with the Soviet Union. The Czech president promised his government "would act in harmony with the Soviet Union in all fields, military, political, economic and cultural".

The Yalta Agreement
Eastern Europeans have seen Yalta as their betrayal by the United States and Britain. Although Stalin agreed to elections in Eastern Europe, the United States and Britain had no power to enforce this.

The Polish elections

The elections in Poland were supposed to take place six months after its liberation. Seeing that the harsh rule of the Soviet Army was insufficient to intimidate the Poles, Stalin decided to delay the elections as long as possible. In the meantime the country was run by a tiny communist group which persecuted non-communists. Millions were accused of collaboration with the Germans and were disqualified from voting in the elections; non-communist candidates were often arrested, especially before the election in 1947. The ruling Communist Party formed an alliance with other parties, and the left-wing members of the Polish Peasant Party (PPP), which was expected to win. In 1946 an election over the abolition of the Polish Senate was rigged and the Senate dismantled. Then in January 1947, the communists and their allies won a truly amazing victory: 394 parliamentary seats compared to the PPP's 28.

Although the United States and Western Europe refused to recognise these falsified results, Stalin asked Boleslaw Bierut, the Polish communist leader, to impose communism on war-devastated Poland. Within a year the PPP was outlawed, Polish socialists were merged with the communists and the Polish Communist Party was purged of any nationalist sympathisers. It now became the ruling party. All factories and industrial enterprises were taken over by the state. The communists began to reorganise land ownership and introduce collectivisation (land belonged to collective farms not private individuals). The Catholic Church was persecuted and all cultural activities were brought under party control. In 1949 Poland became a "People's Democracy" and remained such until 1989.

△ A large pre-election rally is staged in Warsaw, the Polish capital, by the Communist Party and its allies in January 1947. Before the war the Communist Party had about 20,000 members. By the end of 1948, after absorbing the socialists and purging dissenters it claimed to have 1.3 million members.

The Polish terror
The repression in Poland started as soon as the war was over. As former Minister of Agriculture, Stefan Staszewski, said "There is nothing to compare with this period of violence. Not thousands, but tens of thousands of people were killed then. The official trials organised after 1949 were merely an afterword to the extermination of the wartime resistance, of activists, of independent parties and of independent thought in general."

△ Stanislaw Mikolajczyk (right) was the leader of the Polish Peasants' Party. He spent the Second World War in exile in London and was the only exiled leader to return to Poland. When he realised that the communists were manipulating the 1947 elections, he tried to get the elections declared invalid. He failed and was again forced to leave Poland.

▽ Matyas Rakosi of Hungary devised "salami tactics" and oversaw the persecution of his fellow communist leaders during the Stalinist show trials.

The Bulgarians follow suit

In 1945 in Bulgaria, a minute but violent Communist Party formed the Patriotic Front with other political parties. This coalition got 88.2 per cent of the vote, while the previously dominant Peasant Party only received 11 per cent of votes. The Peasant Party was then outlawed and in 1946 another election, this time openly rigged, gave the Communist Party an overwhelming victory. In 1948 Bulgaria became a People's Democracy and remained one of the most Stalinist states until 1989.

"Salami tactics"

In Hungary, where an election was organised in 1945, the Communist Party (CP) did very badly: it polled only 17 per cent of the vote, while the Smallholders' Party got 57 per cent. In spite of this electoral defeat, the communists held all the key posts in the coalition government that ruled the country. The CP then concentrated on undermining the other parties by means of "salami tactics", as the communist leader, Matyas Rakosi, called it. This involved removing opponents "slice by slice" with the co-operation of other members of the coalition government until all opponents were eliminated. Finally in 1947 the Soviet Army, which still occupied the country, arrested a number of non-communist leaders and deported them to Siberia.

Shortly after the arrests another election was held. This time the Smallholders' Party polled only 17 per cent of the vote, while the communist bloc gained the rest. Hungarian social democrats were merged with the CP and in 1949 Hungary became a People's Democracy, and remained so for 40 years.

Romania's experience

During the Second World War Romania was ruled by a fascist dictator, General Ion Antonescu. He sided with the Germans and sent troops to fight against the Soviet Union. At the last minute Romania changed sides and joined the Soviet Army in their struggle against Germany in 1944.

This did not save the country from communism. Early in 1945, the Soviets carried out their first coup against King Michael of Romania, who was forced to appoint a "secret" communist as prime minister. This was followed by rigged elections in 1946. The Democratic Bloc, which was what the insignificant Communist Party called itself, gained 327 seats out of a possible total of 414. In December 1947 the king was forced into exile and the country became a People's Democracy.

Tito seizes power

In Yugoslavia, where Marshal Tito's communist partisans seized power when the occupying German Army withdrew, Serbs, Croats, Slovenes, Macedonians, Voyvodina and Kossovo minorities "voted" overwhelmingly (97 per cent) in a rigged election for Tito's Patriotic Front. This country became a communist ally of the Soviet Union in 1945 and Stalin did not send in troops to prop up the regime. Because Tito came to power without Soviet help, he could afford to take an independent line towards the Soviet Union. Stalin would not tolerate independence and in 1948 had Tito expelled from the Cominform, an international group of communist organisations. Stalin claimed, "If I lift a finger, Tito will fall." However, Tito did not fall. Yugoslavia became a communist non-aligned country which received some support from the west.

Germany

In eastern Germany Stalin could do what he wanted, because the Allies had divided Germany into four occupation zones and he was given a free hand in his own zone. At first he thought that the communists could win a free election in Germany, but in 1946 in Berlin, the Communist Party was severely beaten. The East German Communist Party had to follow the same path as the other Eastern European countries: it was merged with the social democrats and all election results were falsified. By 1949 East Germany was a model People's Democracy and, because of the huge Soviet occupation force, it was one of the Soviet Union's most faithful satellites.

The Yugoslav Civil War
During the Second World War the different nationalities in Yugoslavia took the opportunity to settle old ethnic scores. The Croatian *Ustashas* sided with the Germans and fought against the Serbs. The Serbs divided into the communist partisans and Chetniks, who at first fought together, but later fought each other.

△ Tito in 1956. His real name was Josip Broz and he led the Yugoslav partisans in the fight against the German occupation forces. During the war Tito also engaged in fighting anti-German groups, particularly the Serbian royalists known as the Chetniks. The partisans were able to emerge from the war as the most important political group because they had Stalin's support as well as British backing.

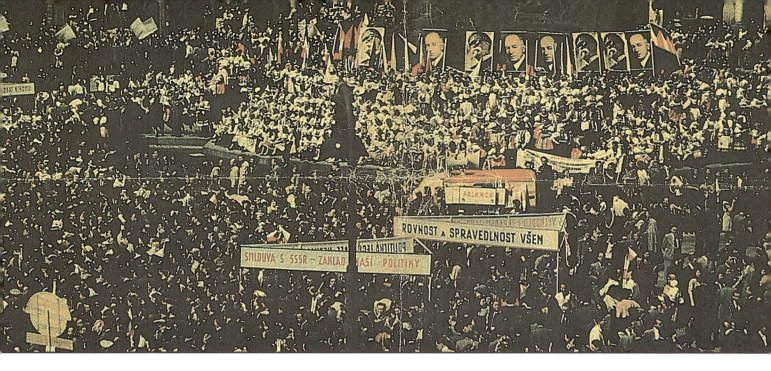

ROVNOST A SPRAVEDLNOST VŠEN

SMLOUVA S SSSR – ZAKLAD ŠAŠI POLITIKY

△ An enormous pro-communist rally in Prague, 1948. In 1946 the Communist Party in Czechoslovakia won over two and half million votes and became the largest party. Many people voted for them because they had not collaborated with the Germans and they promised change.

The communist seizure of power in Czechoslovakia
The Communist Party controlled appointments to the police through its Interior Minister. In February 1948 non-communist ministers protested about this but when nothing happened they offered their resignation. Not all the non-communist ministers resigned, so the communist prime minister was able to stay in power and convince President Beneš to appoint new communist ministers.

The exceptions

Finland and Czechoslovakia both held free elections in 1945 and 1946 respectively. In the former country the Democratic Bloc polled slightly over 30 per cent and shared power in a coalition government with social democrats and conservatives. In the latter the communists polled some 38 per cent of the vote and shared power in a coalition with liberals, socialists and social democrats.

Both countries recovered quickly from the war. However, relations between the superpowers, the United States and the Soviet Union, were deteriorating (this was known as the Cold War). By 1948 the United States and the Soviet Union were determined to maintain their own spheres of influence. Stalin gave a free hand to the Finnish and Czech communist leaders to sort out their internal problems as they pleased as long as they followed the Soviet line.

In Finland the Communist Party failed to dislodge the non-communists from power and the country remained a liberal democracy, increasingly useful to the Soviet Union in international politics as it became more isolated. In Czechoslovakia the communist leaders, encouraged by Stalin, succeeded in gaining power in February 1948. A government crisis occurred when 12 non-communist ministers resigned. The communists, led by Klement Gottwald, then insisted that their own candidates would form the new government. The president, Eduard Beneš, had no choice but to comply since the communists controlled the army, police, secret police and a people's militia made up of communist workers.

Stalinism in Eastern Europe

When communist regimes gained power, they immediately pursued a policy of repression. "Enemies of the people", such as former politicians, Christians, intellectuals, property owners and business people, lost their positions and were "retrained" to work in factories. Some of these "class enemies" were put on trial and sentenced to death. The communist parties of Eastern Europe also went on a recruitment drive to expand their membership and build a base of support within their countries. For example, in Hungary there were thought to be 3,000 communists out of a population of 10 million before the war, but by March 1949 the CP claimed to have 1.2 million members.

However, in 1948 the crisis between Stalin and Tito over Yugoslavia's independent line led to a series of purges within other nations' newly created communist parties. A series of show trials started in Bulgaria, Hungary and other countries. Leaders who were suspect either because of their class background or because they had spent time in Western Europe were made examples of. They were tortured until they confessed to imaginary crimes and then they were sentenced to death to show people what happened to those who were not loyal to the party.

In November 1952 in Czechoslovakia a new element was added: most of the communists on trial were Jewish and they were accused of engineering a Zionist plot against communism. This anti-Semitic accusation was inspired by Soviet advisers to the Czech CP, but there were also many within the secret police willing to scapegoat Jews. The Soviet system was being imposed on Eastern Europe with terror. While Western Europe was trying to rebuild itself after the war, Eastern Europe was building Soviet-style communism where the party was the state and it dominated every sphere of life: work, play and family life.

△ In June 1953 there were riots in Leipzig against the Communist Party. In the photograph above, anti-communists have set fire to a newsstand in the centre of Leipzig.

▽ Hungarian refugees arrive on the Austrian border in 1956. Some 200,000 refugees left Hungary for the west following the uprising.

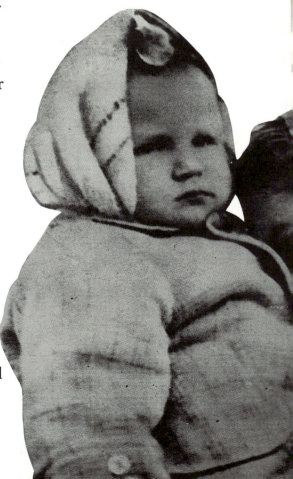

▽ During the Hungarian Uprising protesters tore down the head of Stalin's statue in Budapest. The communist leader of the Hungarian Uprising, Imre Nagy, took refuge in the Yugoslav embassy when the Soviet tanks invaded. After two weeks he came out of hiding after he was told he would not be harmed. He was executed 18 months later along with other leaders.

After Stalin died in 1953, trouble immediately started in Eastern Europe. Three months after Stalin's death the East German government announced very unpopular measures and the workers responded by going on strike. Before the situation could get out of hand the Soviets sent in their troops and at least 21 people were killed. In that year all the satellite countries were shaken by violent mass unrest, but local police forces advised by Soviet experts coped with the disturbances. All the same, the satellite countries adopted new policies and the Soviet Union's economic exploitation of these countries became less blatant.

The Hungarian Uprising

However, in 1956 Poland and Hungary rose again. In June Polish workers came out on strike against working conditions and food shortages. The government sent in tanks and at least 80 people were killed. The disturbances continued, and in October the government collapsed. The Soviet Union threatened to use its army but the Polish CP insisted that Poland should be allowed to sort out its own problems. In 1956 Hungary had severe economic problems and the ruling communists were divided on how to deal with them. After a day of mass demonstrations (23 October) the government collapsed. Imre Nagy became prime minister but the Soviet Union sent tanks in. By 5 November the fighting was over and a communist government faithful to the Soviets had been restored. Hundreds had died.

The Prague Spring

In 1968 it was Czechoslovakia which underwent upheavals. The Czechs and Slovaks wanted to avoid the Hungarian experience and set about trying to reform the CP from within. The CP first secretary, Alexander Dubček, wanted to create "socialism with a human face". Dubček tried to reassure the Soviet leaders that the Czech reforms were not aimed at undermining communism but improving it. Censorship of newspapers, magazines, radio and other media was relaxed, economic reforms were introduced and police control of the state was also dismantled.

People hoped that this new version of communism would work and called it the Prague Spring. But their hopes were short-lived. In August 1968 the Soviet Army restored hardline communism with the force of arms because the Soviet Union did not want an unstable satellite. The Soviet Union installed its own people in power: Gustav Husák became leader of the Communist Party and he brought back many old Stalinists. Although Czech resistance continued for over a year, police repression reinforced by the presence of Soviet troops ensured that Czechoslovakia became a subdued satellite.

The Solidarity movement

In Poland there had been a constant fightback against communism. In 1975-76 Polish tanks were used to kill striking workers, desperately tired of communist economic and political mismanagement. Despite the repression, by 1980 Poland's workers had organised themselves into a powerful social movement along with dissident intellectuals and many Catholics. They had set up their own trade union, known as Solidarity. Workers were again striking nationwide and this time the enfeebled communists did not use tanks. After negotiations Solidarity was allowed to represent Polish workers and Lech Wałęsa emerged as its leader. The Soviet leadership was not happy about this unrest, and in December 1981 General Wojciech Jaruzelski, leader of the CP, was forced by the Soviets to declare martial law. He dissolved Solidarity and imprisoned its leaders. The Soviet leader Leonid Brezhnev wanted no changes in the Stalinist system of power. Solidarity was forced underground but continued to exist and formed its own networks. The other Eastern European countries who had become restless after the success of Polish Solidarity decided there was no point in protesting and suppressed their desire for change.

△ Soviet tanks invade Czechoslovakia in 1968. The tanks were greeted by mass resistance. People set up independent newspapers and radios to keep the spirit of 1968 alive but after a year they were forced to give up.

◁ Lech Wałęsa was a leading member of the strike at the Lenin shipyards in Gdansk in 1980. A well-known speaker, he became leader of the Solidarity trade union and, later, President of Poland.

Charter 77

Protests did continue on a smaller scale. In January 1977 a group of Czech intellectuals set up a human rights movement called Charter 77. Despite the persecution of its leading members, Charter 77 continued its work and provided a focus for resistance to the communist regime. Its first spokesperson, Jan Patočka, died after eight hours of police interrogation. At first the movement documented human rights abuses by the Czech government, but after ten years it broadened its appeal. The playwright Václav Havel became the leading member of Czech resistance.

Widespread repression

It was clear that while the Stalinist communists were in power in the Soviet Union there could be no liberation in Eastern Europe. In fact the widespread working class discontent in Poland forced the other nations to tighten their hold on power.

In the 1980s President Nicolae Ceauşescu of Romania became even more of a tyrant; President Todor Zhivkov of Bulgaria began to persecute intellectuals; President Gustav Husák of Czechoslovakia imprisoned Havel for defamation and exiled rock singers and other so-called criminals such as historians. In Hungary the ageing János Kádár harassed intellectuals; in East Germany the equally ageing Erich Honecker treated his opposition with violence, and shielded himself and his regime behind the Berlin Wall. Paradoxically, Yugoslavia and Albania experienced a certain relaxation in oppression, when their own tyrants, Marshal Tito and Enver Hoxha died.

The Soviet leadership

The communist "nationalists" of Eastern Europe began to despair seeing one old man in the Soviet Union, Brezhnev, succeeded by another, Yuri Andropov, and still another, Konstantin Chernenko. The Eastern European heads of state seemed safe in power forever. Thus the first five years of the 1980s were desolate years for opposition and communist reformers alike.

Then, unexpectedly in 1985, a relatively young man, Mikhail Gorbachev, was elected to the highest party leadership in the Soviet Union. He soon announced that he wanted to change the Soviet system through *perestroika* (restructuring) and *glasnost* (openness) and within five years there have been enormous and rapid changes in the Soviet Union and Eastern Europe.

The collapse of communism

Gorbachev's attempts to reform the Soviet system were a signal to the peoples of Eastern Europe to start their own reforms. But restructuring was not enough for them. They rejected communism entirely.

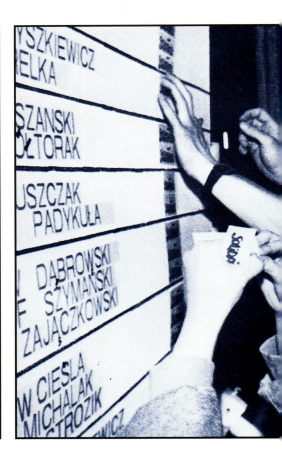

As elsewhere in Eastern Europe the Polish people did not at first realise that Mikhail Gorbachev's accession to power was a significant event. It took the Polish opposition three years to realise its importance and act accordingly.

In April and May 1988 Polish workers went on strike over recognition of the banned trade union, Solidarity. The workers' slogan was "There's no liberty without Solidarity". Only in August of that year, after more strikes, did the communist Interior Minister, General Czeslaw Kiszczak, start negotiations with Lech Wałęsa on the legalisation of Solidarity.

The electoral defeat

After four months of secret negotiations, General Jaruzelski forced the communist leadership to accept the return of Solidarity. By January 1989 the communist state announced that Solidarity was again recognised, and in February talks opened between the communists and Solidarity. They took place at a "round table" and led to the signing of an agreement on 5 April.

In April a law was passed by the *sejm* (Polish parliament), which meant that Solidarity could take part in the legislative elections in June 1989. The Poles were to

△ Delighted Solidarity supporters count up the election results on 6 June 1989. Solidarity won most of the seats it contested.

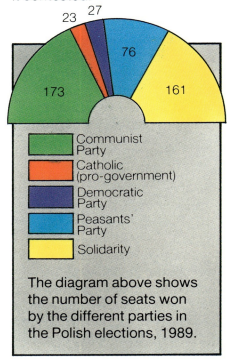

Communist Party — 173
Catholic (pro-government) — 23
Democratic Party — 27
Peasants' Party — 76
Solidarity — 161

The diagram above shows the number of seats won by the different parties in the Polish elections, 1989.

elect a new law-making body, the Senate, and these elections would be absolutely free. For the *sejm* elections, Solidarity was allowed to stand for only 161 seats, while the CP and its allies kept 299 seats through a "reserve list". The communists had made these concessions because the road to democracy was opened once it was clear the Soviets would not intervene. The communist regime in Poland was nearly bankrupt. The only hope was that a Solidarity-backed government might negotiate economic aid from the United States and Western Europe.

In June the election results proved a shock to the communists as Solidarity scored an overwhelming victory: in the Senate it won 99 of the 100 contested seats; in the *sejm* it won all the 161 seats it had stood for. The United Peasants' Party won 76 seats and the Democrats won 27. These parties had been allied with the communists for a long time but they were so impressed by Solidarity's results that they began to speak of collaboration with Solidarity. Shortly after, some Peasants' and Democratic Party deputies dared to vote against General Jaruzelski, who was elected president only by a majority of one, instead of the expected 12.

The Solidarity prime minister

Wałęsa then proposed to the newly elected president that Solidarity form a government, but a communist, General Kiszczak, was given the task. However, this time the Peasants' Party and the Democratic Party openly rebelled against the communists and Kiszczak failed to win a vote of confidence from the *sejm*.

Still Jaruzelski hesitated, unsure of Gorbachev's reaction. But in the end he had to appoint Tadeusz Mazowiecki, a Solidarity leader and editor of the Solidarity newspaper *Gazeta Wyborcza* (*Election Gazette*), as prime minister. Mazowiecki was careful and allowed the communists to keep the ministries of defence and interior, but otherwise Solidarity and its allies held a majority of the posts in the coalition government.

For the first time since the war Poland was led by a non-communist prime minister backed by a majority in the *sejm*. It was free to launch a reform programme which would put Poland back on the road to recovery and future prosperity. In the meantime Poland served as an example to the neighbouring communist states. If Poland could elect a non-communist government why not the other Eastern European countries?

▽ Following Solidarity's success in the 1989 elections, Tadeusz Mazowiecki became the first non-communist prime minister in Eastern Europe.

The Hungarian experiment

Though Hungarian communists had started experimenting with liberal economic reforms as far back as 1968, and more radically in 1984, while János Kádár was in power, these reforms did not go far enough and problems grew. Above all Hungary borrowed huge amounts of money from Western Europe to keep the existing communist system going, and faced a deepening economic crisis. However, by 1989 Kádár had retired and his successor, Károly Grósz, was under pressure from radicals. He was forced to announce increasingly more dramatic changes, such as holding talks with opposition parties in order to fend off reformers and pacify public opinion.

In June 1989, the leader of the 1956 uprising, Imre Nagy, and his associates were reburied with full honours. Although leading members of the Communist Party were present, the ceremony was a moving national event. Kádár, the man who sent Nagy to death, was nowhere to be seen and in fact died three weeks later. A week after Nagy's funeral, following the changes in Poland, the Hungarian reformers forced Grósz to convene an extraordinary congress and to share power with three other leaders. For the next few months the Communist Party held talks with the opposition parties, rather like the Polish round table talks. On 18 September an agreement was signed which outlined various changes, including the holding of free parliamentary elections.

To face these elections, the Communist Party got rid of all its "compromised leaders", including Grosz, and proclaimed its aim was not communism but social democracy. The elections were held in March 1990 and the right-wing Democratic Forum party took power as head of a coalition government. It immediately set about ambitious reforms to install a full free-market system through privatisation and modernisation of industry.

Strangely enough, it was one of Hungary's earliest radical measures which set off the fall of the East German communist regime. In 1989, the Hungarians took away the barbed wire barriers from its border with Austria. East German tourists in Hungary used the open border to flee to West Germany. When the East German leader Erich Honecker asked Hungary to close the border, another exodus started through Czechoslovakia where the government had to arrange special trains to take refugees to the West.

△ After the Hungarian Uprising in 1956, János Kádár became the Hungarian leader of the Communist Party. He hung on to power for 20 years and during this time introduced many reforms.

△ Kádár's successor as leader of the Hungarian Communist Party, Károly Grósz, did not last very long in power. After over a year he was dropped by the party as it faced elections in March 1990.

The communists give up

In October Honecker celebrated the 40th anniversary of the founding of the German Democratic Republic. While Honecker and Gorbachev greeted each other, a refugee train passing through Dresden provoked serious rioting in that city. There was increasing public restlessness, particularly in Leipzig. Honecker responded by ordering the security forces to disperse demonstrations.

By then Honecker and his government knew that they could not rely on the help of Soviet military forces. They were divided about what to do. Honecker favoured a military solution, but Egon Krenz, in charge of security, suppressed the order to use violence against the crowds. One night demonstrators were brutally beaten up, arrested and sentenced to imprisonment. But the next day some 70,000 people were allowed to make a peaceful protest. Honecker was dismissed and there followed resignations and expulsions from the Communist Party. For a month Krenz was the head of state and general secretary of the Communist Party. He appointed as prime minister Hans Modrow, the party chief for the Dresden region and a known reformer. On 9 November Krenz allowed his border guards to open the Berlin Wall. East Germans could now travel freely to the other Germany. Then in December 1989 the party elected a new leader, Gregor Gysi, changed its name and expelled all the compromised leaders, including Krenz. It also agreed to hold a free election.

△ Erich Honecker, the former leader of East Germany, has recently been arrested because of his connections with the East German secret police, the Stasi. However, due to illness, he may never be sentenced.

▽ A demonstration in Leipzig during the run-up to the elections in March 1990. Since the summer of 1989 crowds demonstrated in Leipzig every Monday. At first they were small gatherings, but by November over 100,000 people demanded political reforms.

Free elections

The marches in Leipzig continued every Monday throughout the crisis until they were so large it was difficult to know their size: it is estimated that between 300,000 and half a million took part. This put pressure on Modrow's communist-dominated government to put through more liberal measures. The political police, known as the Stasi, was dissolved by the government and then its headquarters were sacked by demonstrators, while calls for the reunification of the two Germanys became more frequent in the demonstrating crowds. The slogan changed from "Wir sind das Volk" ("We are the people") to "Wir sind ein Volk" ("We are one nation").

In the end Modrow had to call for a coalition government with the opposition so that East Germany could survive peacefully until the election, which was held on 18 March 1990. During the election campaign the issue of German reunification took priority and the West German-backed Christian Democrats, who favoured early reunification, won a resounding victory.

The undignified collapse of communism in East Germany had a most powerful effect on its neighbour, Czechoslovakia. The domino theory that one collapsing communist state would cause another to fall was at last being confirmed.

The new Czechoslovak leader

As soon as Gorbachev launched *perestroika* and *glasnost* in the Soviet Union, he put pressure on the Czechoslovak leaders to reform communism in their country. Gorbachev let it be known that he was critical of the Soviet Union's invasion of Czechoslovakia in 1968. In 1987, Miloš Jakeš was made first secretary of the Czech Communist Party but all the other leaders remained in power.

They introduced very little change, although in 1988 Soviet pressure began to bear fruit. Jakeš purged the government and Ladislav Adamec became prime minister. He was an experienced Communist Party member and was known to be a reformer. However Jakeš also promoted some old-style Stalinists, known as hardliners, like Miroslav Štěpán and the rising youth leader, Vasil Mohorita. Throughout 1988-89 Prime Minister Adamec talked reform, particularly when abroad, but at home the hardliners blocked the passage of any reforms. Compared to the Soviet Union, Czechoslovakia was not introducing any "democratic" changes.

△ During the demonstrations in October and November 1989, Václav Havel emerged as a leader of anti-communist opposition. He had spent many years in jail under the communists and although he was well-known in Prague, he was not known in the rest of Czechoslovakia. Other leaders also emerged including the dissident priest, Václav Malý, and the singer Marta Kubišová. At one point, the leader of the Prague Spring in 1968, Alexander Dubček, joined Havel on a balcony in Wenceslas Square. The opposition leaders formed themselves into Civic Forum and launched a nationwide setting up of organisations to take over power from the communists.

The student protest

The year 1989 started badly for Jakeš' hardline leadership. In January 1989 special riot police dispersed a mass demonstration commemorating the death of Jan Palach, who had burned himself to death in 1969 in protest against the Soviet invasion. There was rioting in May and October, but the specially trained anti-riot troops seemed capable of controlling the situation. The party leaders heaved a sigh of relief and regained confidence.

Nonetheless, Gorbachev was far from satisfied and in November he told the Czechoslovak leaders that the Soviet Union would publicly condemn the 1968 invasion. Even though the neighbouring German communist regime was collapsing, Jakeš thought the riot police could control mass demonstrations. This false sense of security led him to authorise a demonstration on 17 November 1989 to commemorate the students who had demonstrated against the Nazi occupation 50 years earlier.

Immense crowds (some estimate 50,000) gathered in a suburb and heard official speakers praise the students' sacrifice in 1939. However, after the ceremony, a large number of students decided to march to Wenceslas Square to have their own commemoration. As they marched to the city centre, many onlookers joined in. Jakeš and Štěpán told the police authorities not to allow the students into Wenceslas Square and the riot police clashed with demonstrators and beat many of them brutally. Some 293 students were seriously injured.

The mass exodus
In the summer of 1989, East German tourists in Hungary began to use the border with Austria to travel to West Germany. This movement of refugees accelerated after the East German communist leader, Erich Honecker, asked Hungary to close its borders. East German tourists in Czechoslovakia rushed to the West German Embassy in Prague and claimed political asylum. The Czechoslovak government then arranged special trains to take the refugees to West Germany.

▽ On 28 November 1989, 10,000 people demonstrated in Wenceslas Square in Prague, demanding free elections. The opposition leaders formed themselves into Civic Forum and won the June 1991 elections. Havel became president of Czechoslovakia.

△ Milos Jakeš became first secretary of the Czech Communist Party in 1987. His authorisation of a demonstration that resulted in violence, eventually led to the formation of the Civic forum and the ultimate election of Václav Havel as president.

Bulgaria's future

Bulgaria is one of the poorest countries in Europe, and the problems it faces are immense. There are widespread shortages of such necessities as milk, cheese, eggs, meat and vegetables. Productivity in industry is low and the quality of goods produced is poor. Petrol is in short supply and there are constant power cuts. It has a $7 billion foreign debt, on which it cannot pay any interest. The new leaders will have to get help from the European Community in order to rebuild the economy and provide people with basic goods. However, Bulgaria is one of many countries asking for aid.

The "peaceful" revolution

On 18 November fantastic rumours circulated in Prague about police brutality and student casualties. Crowds formed spontaneously and the people marched to Wenceslas Square. This time the police did not respond with violence because the crowds were too big.

On 24 November Jakeš convened an emergency session of the central committee to deal with the crisis. However, this was irrelevant, for power was in the streets with the crowds and their leaders. The crowds soon found their leader, the dissident playwright Václav Havel. In a state of panic Prime Minister Adamec announced a "new" government on 3 December, which still had a communist majority. The demonstrations continued and Adamec resigned. By 11 December the Slovak communist leader, Marián Čalfa, became prime minister and his government had a non-communist majority. President Husák resigned and on 29 December Václav Havel was elected as his successor. The revolution was complete, without any shedding of blood; it was called the "tender" (or velvet) revolution because it happened so smoothly.

For Czechoslovakia it means that the wheel of history has been turned back to democracy which it had from 1918-38 and from 1945-48. The election in June 1990 brought in a coalition government grouped around the former opposition Civic Forum.

Bulgaria

Amid all the upheavals in Eastern Europe, Todor Zhivkov, in power in Bulgaria since 1954, seemed a tower of strength. However, this power was a facade and his corrupt rule came to a swift end after a tiny demonstration in the capital city of Sofia in November 1989. He was toppled from power by a reformist, Petar Mladenov. A week after Zhivkov's fall, 50,000 people marched peacefully through Sofia asking for democracy, free elections and Zhivkov's trial. The first free elections were held in June 1990 and resulted in the return of the Bulgarian Socialist Party (the former Communists) to power. However, support for the Bulgarian Socialist Party declined, and after internal disagreements in the party a new – wholly non-communist – government was formed in November 1991. Like many other Eastern European countries, Bulgaria now faces frightening economic problems – in 1991, the output from industry fell by nearly 25 per cent, exports plummetted and unemployment soared.

The fall of Ceauşescu

The former leader of Romania, Nicolae Ceauşescu, ran Romania for 24 years through his family members, who held all key government posts. There were widespread food and energy shortages because he exported domestic food products to repay all of Romania's foreign debts. He also pursued a policy of persecuting the Hungarian minority in Transylvania. Despite these evident difficulties at home, the Ceauşescu family members were re-elected by a Communist Party congress in November 1989. Oppression was so severe that there was little visible opposition.

However there was unrest in Romania. On 18 December Ceauşescu ordered the suppression of a demonstration in Timisoara over the arrest of an obscure dissident pastor, Laszlo Tökés. The communist political police, known as the Securitate, arrested, tortured and executed hundreds of Timisoara citizens. Although similar unrest all over the country was reported to him, Ceauşescu did not take the reports seriously. On his return from a visit to Teheran, a huge crowd outside his palace in Bucharest suddenly began to chant "Ceauşescu, assassin" and he lost his nerve. Before fleeing with his wife, Elena, he ordered the Securitate to fire into the crowd. At this point the Romanian Army switched sides and tried to protect the demonstrators. Nonetheless in the ensuing fighting some 800 people were shot dead.

While the tyrant and his wife were on the run the fight for power between the army and Securitate went on. The fighting was particularly bad in Bucharest, where it was shown, hour by hour, on State Television. Then, on Christmas Day, television showed the trial and execution of the Ceauşescus. All Romanians saw their rulers dead on television and knew that their revolution was won.

The National Salvation Front was formed immediately the Ceauşescu couple left the palace. Dominated by communist leaders who had fallen foul of the dictator – Ion Iliescu and Silviu Brucan – the NSF started a programme of reforms promising better food supplies, more petrol and energy, and held free multi-party elections in May 1990. The NSF was voted into power but its reforms have been slowed down by strikes, protests and demonstrations over massive price rises and unemployment. The events in Romania showed that there could be no military solution to people power. The consequences of Ceauşescu's misrule will take years to put right, and the west will have to help Romania on its road to democracy.

▽ Nicolae Ceauşescu and his wife, Elena, were shown on television shortly before they were executed. The Securitate stopped fighting the army soon after their deaths.

Albania

Despite the dramatic events in Eastern Europe, Albania has been relatively calm. Hoxha's successor, Ramiz Alia, tried to keep the old Stalinist system. But food riots, strikes and the flight of thousands of Albanian refugees to Italy and Greece forced the liberalisation of the constitution. Elections in March 1991 brought the Albanian Party of Labour (renamed communists) to power. Public unrest continued, however, and the government fell in June 1991. The government, returned to power in the March 1992 elections, must face and deal with what is arguably the most backward of all Eastern Europe's economies – first among its priorities will be severe food shortages.

Yugoslavia

The federation of six states that made up Yugoslavia was held together only by totalitarian communist rule. When that was removed, in the elections of 1991, Yugoslavia started to shake itself apart. The states of Slovenia and Croatia, which were relatively prosperous, voted for democracy and independence. But the Serbian communists, led by Slobodan Milosevic, wanted the Yugoslav federation to remain as before – and be dominated by Serbia.

What started as minor violent clashes between Serbs and Croats developed into a bitter, bloody civil war in 1991. As the fighting became ever more violent, so the worries of the rest of Europe increased. The EC negotiated ceasefires with all sides, but none held for more than a few days. In the second half of 1991, many feared the conflict would spread to Romania and other neighbours.

UN intervention had limited success. A ceasefire was declared due largely to Milosevic's growing realisation that Serbia's economic plight was desperate. Hyper-inflation reached 3,000 per cent, and an embargo on essential trade with the EC and USA had been imposed.

A UN peacekeeping force arrived in 1992 to police the ceasefire between the Serbs and Croats. But elsewhere, further fighting flared up with even greater violence in the state of Bosnia Hercegovina, centred on Sarajevo. The Muslim population came under heavy attack from Christian Serbs and Montenegrans. Muslim towns and villages were "ethnically cleansed", leaving tens of thousands homeless. UN efforts have focused on attempts to provide humanitarian aid by truck and air. But all attempts at peace negotiations have failed so far.

△ Crowds of Serbian nationalists demonstrate against Albanian demands for self-rule in Kossovo, March 1989. This is a pressing problem facing Yugoslavia.

The Future

Most Eastern European countries are finding the advent of democracy and the free-market system difficult to cope with. Despite the lack of freedom, life was more stable for the ordinary people under communism: food was subsidised and there was plenty of work.

Now unemployment is growing in all Eastern European countries and the price of food, and other goods, is going up. Public protests against these hardships have forced a slow-down of reform in some countries. But it is unlikely that there will be a return to the old "command economies" and repression of the Stalinist system.

The break-up of the Soviet Union into the Commonwealth of Independent States means that the whole of the formerly communist Eastern and Central Europe has now taken the road to democracy and the capitalist free-market system. To push them further along this path, the countries of Eastern Europe are forging ever stronger links with Western Europe, particularly the European Community which is sending financial and technical aid into the East.

In 1991 Western and Eastern Germany became one nation again – a nation with a social and economic base firmly in the EC.

Hungary is already an associate member of the EC and has announced its intention of becoming a full member by 1996. Similarly, Poland and Czechoslovakia have expressed the desire to join the EC.

But there are many obstacles to be overcome before the countries of Eastern Europe can become full and equal members of Western Europe. Nationalism is present in different degrees in all countries. In Yugoslavia it caused a violent civil war. In the eastern part of the new Germany it is responsible for an increasing number of racial attacks on foreigners and refugees. In Czechoslovakia there is growing rivalry between the Czechs and Slovaks, and Havel has resigned. Hungary has set an example by trying to tackle the problems of ethnic minorities – Croats, Romanians, Slovaks and Slovenes – through consultation with them.

Eastern Europe has chosen democracy and the free-market. But it is now finding that the change from the communist system is far from easy. However, Western Europe has never been more stable and prosperous and willing to help its eastern neighbours share in that peace and prosperity.

▽ One of the consequences of the civil war raging in Yugoslavia. This building in Sarajevo, Bosnia, has been reduced to a blackened shell after repeated mortar attacks.

Eastern Europe

Former East Germany

East Germany was created from the zone of Germany occupied by the Soviet Army after 1945. It has a population of 16,646,000 of whom 99.7 per cent are German. Its surface area is 41,645 sq miles (107,860 sq km). A quarter of this area is covered by forests. Although it lacks many raw materials, it is a highly industrialised country. It specialises in producing machinery and chemicals as well as textiles, clothing, glass and china. Its main source of power is brown coal. Its agriculture is efficient and modern but relies too much on fertilisers.

Poland

Following the Second World War Poland got a third of its present territory from Germany, namely East Prussia and Silesia. It has 37,864,000 inhabitants, of whom a very small percentage are Ukrainians and Germans. Its area is 120,348 sq miles (311,700 sq km). It has large reserves of coal, copper, zinc and other raw materials. It is a major world producer of brown coal and along the Baltic coast it has huge shipyards. However its agriculture is backward and its economy is in chaos because Poland is crippled by foreign debt.

Czechoslovakia

It is made up of Bohemia and Moravia (the Czech republic) and Slovakia. It has 15,604,000 inhabitants of whom 30 per cent are Slovaks. There are also Hungarians, Poles, Germans, Ukrainians and others living within its borders. It has a total area of 49,371 sq miles (127,870 sq km). Only 12 per cent of its territory is lowlands. It possesses many raw materials, including coal, and uranium. It has a highly developed industry and efficient agriculture. It exports glass, china, machines, leather goods, clothing and wooden products.

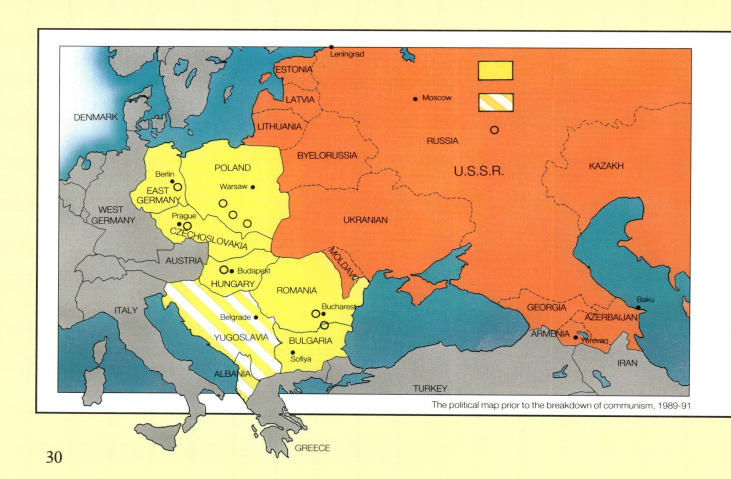

The political map prior to the breakdown of communism, 1989-91

Romania

Romania is surrounded by the Carpathian Mountains. It has a population of 23,014,000. Some 7.3 per cent are Hungarians and 9.9 per cent are of other nationalities including German. Its surface area is 91,699 sq miles (237,500 sq km). It has vast deposits of natural gas, oil and rock salt but its industry is not highly developed. It does produce some machinery and chemicals. For over 20 years Ceauşescu followed a policy of exporting goods which meant the people did not have enough to eat but Romania had no foreign debts.

Bulgaria

Bulgaria has a long history of Turkish rule. It has a total population of 8,982,000 and has a sizeable Turkish minority (8.5 per cent). From 1984 onwards the government forced the Turks to assimilate and thousands have left for Turkey. Its total surface is 42,823 sq miles (110,912 sq km). It is a very mountainous country. It is not a highly industrialised country. It exports agricultural produce, some machinery, metals and chemicals. It also produces textiles and tobacco. It imports industrial goods, fuel and raw materials.

Hungary

Hungary has 80 per cent of its land in the Great Plain of the Danube which has a rich, loamy soil and is excellent for agriculture. It has a population of 10,647,000 consisting mainly of Hungarians, but also small minorities of Germans, Slovaks and others. Its area is 35,919 sq miles (93,030 sq km). It has coal deposits, some iron and copper as well as bauxite. It has developed engineering and light industries with some success but is crippled by foreign debts. Its main products are transport equipment, electrical goods, aluminium, food and wine.

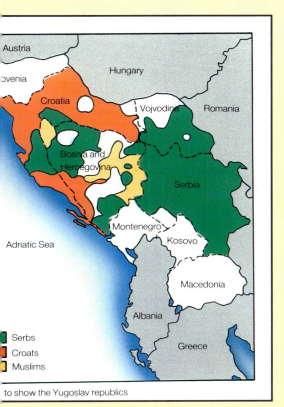

Serbs

Croats

Muslims

to show the Yugoslav republics

Yugoslavia

Yugoslavia is a federation of six republics: Slovenia, Croatia, Bosnia and Hercegovina, Serbia, Montenegro and Macedonia. It has 23,273,000 inhabitants and is made up of many different ethnic groups. These include Albanians, Bulgarians, Romanians, Slovaks and Turks. Its surface is 98,766 sq miles (255,804 sq km). Yugoslavia has rich mineral ores: copper, zinc, lead, aluminium, antimony and mercury, but its economy is very unstable.

Albania

Albania is a small mountainous country. It has a population of 3,149,000 and has a small number of Greeks, gypsies and other nationalities. It has an area of 111,000 sq miles (28,748 sq km). It has a backward economy though it does have food, textiles, petroleum, mining and timber industries. Its major products are oil, bitumen, metals (chrome, nickel and copper), tobacco, fruit and vegetables. Its government has restricted relations with the outside world.

The economic background

Since the Second World War Eastern Europe has been dominated by the Soviet Union economically. After the war the Soviet Union seized control of many factories from Eastern European countries.

The command economy

The communist regimes in Eastern Europe nationalised industry so that all factories belonged to the state. The economies were planned, that is, the government told all the factories what and how much they should produce. There was great emphasis on increasing output of heavy industry, such as steel and engineering. Land was also taken over by the state and organised into collective farms. Prices of goods were subsidised and little attention was paid to what people wanted to buy. Everyone had a job but wages were low. There was cheap housing and people could buy food at subsidised prices. Saving money was easy

Pollution problems

The fall of the communist governments of Eastern Europe has exposed serious ecological problems. In East Germany 70 per cent of energy requirements are met by burning brown coal, which produces noxious fumes. Some 66 per cent of rivers need cleaning, and heavy use of fertilisers has damaged the soil. A recent report suggested that 83 per cent of East Germany's forests are damaged by acid rain. East Germany imports toxic waste from West Germany.

In Czechoslovakia there are similar problems. Again most energy requirements are met by burning brown coal, which produces sulphur dioxide pollution. Some 70 per cent of its rivers are polluted by mining wastes, nitrates, manure and oil. About 50 per cent of the forests are dying. The Czech government sees the answer to the ecological problems as building nuclear power stations to cut down on sulphur dioxide emissions.

Poland is probably the most polluted country in Europe. It uses brown coal to produce energy, and sulphur dioxide pollution is extremely bad in Upper Silesia and Krakow. Nuclear power stations were being built but the nuclear power programme has now been frozen. Many vegetables grown in polluted areas have metal deposits. There are severe health problems in badly polluted areas.

Hungary has a major sulphur dioxide problem but it gets most of its energy from oil and gas power stations. Much of its water is unfit for drinking and most of the population do not have sewage facilities. It stores toxic waste from the west.

Romania gets most of its electricity from oil and gas so it has no problem with sulphur dioxide. However 84 per cent of water is unfit to drink and there is a deforestation problem.

Bulgaria does not have problems with sulphur dioxide but it gets air pollution from Romanian factories. Some of its mountains are becoming deforested and the Black Sea is heavily polluted.

Eastern Europe needs help to tackle these environmental problems, but they may take second place to sorting out economic problems.

but there was nothing to buy. In 1945 the countries of Eastern Europe all had different histories in terms of economic development. They have grown at different rates. East Germany and Czechoslovakia had the most advanced industries in 1939 and this remains the case.

The Polish system

When communism was first introduced to Poland, the standard of living of workers in the cities dropped. Following strikes and unrest in 1956, the Polish government got the Soviet Union's agreement that the collectivisation of agriculture could be abandoned and the industrialisation programme was slowed down.

In 1970 the government tried to cut price subsidies. Again there were strikes and the government backed down. This happened again in 1976 and in 1980. The net result of this is that food prices are kept low to keep the factory workers happy, but farmers are not paid enough for their labour so agriculture declines.

Goulash communism

After the uprising in 1956 in Hungary, the communist leadership was given a free hand on how to run the country. The system it embarked on (a mixture of free market and state control) was called goulash communism.

The result was successful up to a point: there were goods in the shops and consumers were happy. But a black market developed and people had to take on two or even three jobs to keep up their standard of living. Some people did very well, such as private entrepreneurs, doctors and crafts people.

Then in the 1980s things went wrong. Foreign trade did not bring in as much money and imports became more expensive. The Hungarian government borrowed money from the west to keep the country going. Inflation rose to 20 per cent in the 1970s and incomes dropped.

COMECON

The Eastern Bloc countries were part of an economic alliance with the Soviet Union known as COMECON (Council for Mutual Economic Assistance). With the liberalisation of their economies and the break-up of the Soviet Union, Comecon was dissolved in June 1991. Comecon used to guarantee trade between its members and now these guarantees are gone, some countries found their exports disappeared almost overnight.

Privatisation

All East European countries are allowing private ownership of formerly state-run concerns – from tiny restaurants to huge factories. Hungary and Czechoslovakia are ahead of the others, but sometimes buyers for such concerns cannot be found because they cannot be made to make a profit.

▽ The maps below show how energy and mineral resources are distributed throughout the East European countries.

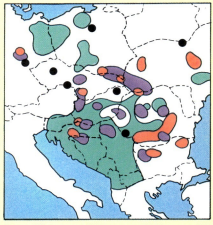

Energy resources

🟥	Oil fields
🟪	Natural gas fields
🟩	Coal fields
●	Major Nuclear and Hydro electric power stations

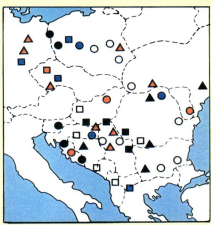

Mineral resources

🔴	Gold
🔵	Silver
⚫	Lead
⚪	Zinc
🟥	Tin
⬛	Iron Ore
🟦	Nickel
⬜	Bauxite
🔺	Copper
▲	Uranium

Chronology

For centuries Eastern Europe has been inhabited by different groups of the Slavonic or Slavic peoples. They drifted into Europe, forced to move by warriors from the east. They all developed their own languages and cultures but few gained independence. The Turks threatened to overrun the area before being defeated in 1683. The rule of the three empires brought stability, but the breakdown of that system led to the First World War. Many of the countries we know as Eastern Europe became recognised nations after the First World World War.

1914 The First World War begins. Austria-Hungary is in alliance with Germany against Russia, Britain and France.

1917 The Russian Revolution takes place. The communists seize power.

1918 End of the First World War. Germany and Austria-Hungary surrender.

1919 The Treaty of Versailles is signed in France. New states are created in Eastern Europe: Czechoslovakia and Yugoslavia. Poland and Hungary become independent. Romania and Bulgaria have new borders.

1938 German troops go into Austria and annex it. Hitler gets the Sudetenland from Czechoslovakia.

1939 Hitler occupies the rest of Czechoslovakia and makes Slovakia into a puppet state. Hitler and the Soviet leader Stalin sign the Nazi-Soviet Pact and agree to divide up Poland between them. Hitler invades Poland and the Second World War begins. Germany is at war with Britain and France.

1941 Hitler invades the Soviet Union. The Soviet Union joins the Allies: Britain and France.

1945 The Soviet Army defeats Germany in the east and takes Berlin. Soviet armies occupy Eastern Europe and a communist government is set up in Poland.

1946 Hungary, Bulgaria and Albania become republics.

1947 Romania becomes a republic. Communists gain power in Hungary.

1948 Communists seize power in Czechoslovakia, Romania, Bulgaria and Poland.

1948-49 West and East Germany established as separate states.

1953 Stalin dies and Khrushchev becomes the new party leader in the Soviet Union. Anti-communist riots in East Germany.

1955 The Soviet Union signs the Warsaw Pact with its Eastern European "allies".

1956 Anti-communist unrest in Poland is suppressed by Polish government. The Soviets put down the Hungarian Uprising.

1961 East German government builds the Berlin Wall.

1968 The Prague Spring: the Czech Communist Party tries to reform communism. In August Soviet tanks invade Czechoslovakia.

1970 Unrest in Poland over price reform.

1980 Strikes in Poland, led by the trade union Solidarity.

1981 Martial law declared in Poland.

1985 Gorbachev becomes Soviet leader.

1986 Nuclear reactor disaster at Chernobyl in the Soviet Union.

1989 Poland has partially free elections and gets a non-communist prime minister and a Solidarity government. Hungary's Communist Party agrees to hold free elections. East Germans leave for the west and there are massive anti-communist demonstrations. The East German Communist Party loses its leading role in the state and the Berlin Wall is opened. Czechoslovakia gets a non-communist president. Zhivkov of Bulgaria is sacked by the Communist Party. Ceauşescu falls from power in Romania.

1990 Free elections held in most countries in Eastern Europe.

1991-92 Civil war breaks out in Yugoslavia between Croatians, Serbians and Bosnians. Czechoslovakia opts for split into two separate nations.

Glossary

Anti-Semitism is the hostility to Jewish people. It has its historic origins in religious intolerance and economic jealousy. It was common throughout Eastern Europe and was a policy of the Russian emperors in the 19th century and of Hitler in the 20th century.

Cold War was the period of strained relations between the United States and the Soviet Union after 1945. It has lasted on and off but diminished in intensity in 1985 when Gorbachev came to power.

Collectivisation is the redistribution of land so that it is run by a collective farm. Teams of farm workers rather than individuals or families plough, plant and harvest crops.

Cominform was the international organisation set up by Stalin to try to foster world revolution.

Communism is the belief that all private wealth should be abolished and should be held in common, that is, by the state. In practice the state decides who has money and fixes prices.

Democracy is a political system where people have a say in choosing or electing their government.

Ethnic is the word used to describe different peoples or nations.

Fascism has come to mean anyone with extreme right-wing views. It was used to describe the German and Italian regimes of the 1930s.

First World War was fought from 1914-18. It was the first of two great European wars in the 20th century. The Allies (Britain, France, Russia, and later Italy and the United States) fought the Central Powers (Germany, the Austro-Hungarian empire joined by Turkey). The Allies won.

Glasnost is the Russian word meaning transparency or openness which is used to describe the cultural and political openness in the Soviet Union under Gorbachev.

Hardliner is the term used to describe the communist leaders who do not want any change in the communist system.

Nationalism is the belief that individual communities or cultures – usually defined by a common language – should be independent and self-determining rather than part of an empire.

National Socialism or **Nazism** was the racial doctrine expounded by Hitler in Germany in the 1920s. It was a mixture of nationalism and socialism; Hitler promised to build up Germany as a nation and made promises about looking after workers' interests.

Parliament is a law-making body. In a democracy it is elected by the people.

Partisans were guerrilla fighters of the resistance in European states, such as Yugoslavia. They were often members of the socialist and communist opposition to fascism.

Perestroika is the Russian word for restructuring. It is used to describe Soviet attempts to reform the communist system.

Satellite is the term used to describe those countries which are economically and politically dependent on a more powerful country.

Second World War lasted from 1939-45. It was fought between the Axis powers (Germany, Italy and Japan) and the Allies (the United States, the Soviet Union, Britain, France and others). It ended with the defeat of Japan and Germany and the division of Europe.

Soviet originally meant a workers' council. Now it is used to describe the Soviet Union.

Stalinism was the form of communism developed by the Soviet leader Josef Stalin. It meant brutal repression of the anti-communist opposition by the secret police. In economic terms it meant emphasis on increasing production of heavy industry and collectivising land.

Treaty of Versailles was signed at the end of the First World War by Germany and the Allies.

Warsaw Pact is a defence treaty agreeing to mutual military help, signed by the Soviet Union, Poland, Czechoslovakia, East Germany, Hungary, Romania and Bulgaria.

Zionism is the belief held by some Jewish people that they have biblical rights to a homeland in Israel.

Index

Photographic Credits:
Cover, back cover and pages 23 top, 26, 28-29 bottom: Frank Spooner Pictures; intro page: Toni Nemes; pages 6 both, 8 bottom, 9, 10-11, 12, 13 both, 14, 15, 16 both, 18 top, 21 bottom, 22 both, 24, 25, 27, 28-29 top: Topham Picture Source and Associated Press; page 8 top, 17, 18 bottom, 20-21 top: Popperfoto; page 23 bottom: Michael Hughes.